CHEROPHOBIA:

CONFESSIONS OF A LOVESICK YOUNG ADULT

Jada L. Hollingsworth

Wider Perspectives Publishing ∞ 2024 ∞ Hampton Roads, Va.

The poems and writings in this book are the creations and property of Jada Lasha Hollingsworth, the author is responsible for them as such. Wider Perspectives Publishing reserves 1st run rights to this material in this form, all rights revert to author upon delivery. Author reserves all rights thereafter: Do not reproduce, distribute or transmit without Author's written permission except Fair Use practices for approved promotion or educational purposes. Author may redistribute, whole or in part, at will, for example submission to anthologies or contests.

Scriptural quotations are from the New International Version of the Bible.

©2025, Jada L. Hollingsworth
1st run complete in September 2025
Wider Perspectives Publishing, Hampton Roads, Va.
ISBN   978-1-964531-90-8

DEDICATED TO

MY SON, WHO TAUGHT ME WHAT TRUE LOVE IS.

GABBY, FOR BEING MY EDITOR AND BETA READER

MY MOM FOR BEING THE BEST MARKETER EVER

AND TO MICHAEL JUDGE FOR PUSHING ME TO WRITE THESE BOOKS IN THE FIRST PLACE.
THIS BOOK IS FOR YOU.

1 Corinthians 13:4-8 NIV

Love is patient, love is kind. It does not envy, it does not boast, it is not proud. It does not dishonor others, it is not self-seeking, it is not easily angered, and it keeps no record of wrongs. Love does not delight in evil but rejoices with the truth. It always protects, always trusts, always hopes, always perseveres. Love never fails. But where there are prophecies, they will cease; where there are tongues, they will be stilled; where there is knowledge, it will pass away.

INTRODUCTION

These poems are about love life and dreams of the future. In my family, the most important thing after your education was having a partner. In elementary school, everyone would ask me if I had a crush on anyone or if I had a boyfriend. I had come to this flawed realization that my family would value me more if I had a partner. I would be more whole of a person if I were in a relationship.

I named this book Cherophobia because through therapy and finding myself in adulthood, I have realized that one of the reasons I stay in toxic relationships is that I am afraid to be happy. I felt like true happiness was something that I did not deserve. I also tend to be a bit of a pessimist. If things are going well with someone, I wait for the other shoe to drop instead of enjoying being happy.

This was my first relationship after being abused for years, so I know it must not have been easy for him, either. I was actively in therapy, but while we were together, I was diagnosed with PTSD, borderline personality disorder, and bipolar disorder. As much as we cared for each other, there was nothing we could have done to make our relationship work. He was chasing his dreams as a musician, and I was still trying to figure out who I was. We were in two separate phases of life. Being the person that I am now, looking back at this relationship, I wish I had met him later in life. He was pivotal in healing my traumas and becoming the prolific writer that I am today, but I cannot help but feel like the Jada that I am now would have been perfect for him, but it's too late.

There is no greater pain than a soulmate lost. You can notice in this series how my writing changed from being light and jovial to dark and moody to now being a blissful joy that transitions into tales of sadness, disappointment, and true loss. I am immensely proud of this collection of works. The trials of my life and becoming a single mom pushed me away from writing for years. After a conversation with God, the love of a lifetime, and three long years of struggling to find myself again, I produced this book.

Working through this series has shown me how far I have come as a woman and writer. Based on that alone, they needed to be shared. So, I hope you enjoy them. Feel free to aww, cringe, laugh, reminisce. and take pity as you flow through the Confessions of a Lovesick Young Adult.

Cherophobia ~
The fear of being happy

Cherophobia: Confessions of a Lovesick Young Adult

Jada's Prayer

God, I am looking for a man
after your own heart, like David
A man that will not break my heart,
but save it

Happy with themselves
And loves their life
But honestly still
Wants a wife

Driven and ambitious
Moving with a purpose
Someone who will work for my love
Show me they deserve it

Respectful and considerate
God-fearing and kind
Shows me with consistency
that I am on their mind

Someone that knows
what they want out of living
Pursuing their passions
Their gift keeps on giving

Financially stable,
can head a home
Treats me like his Queen,
upon a throne

Friendly and cheerful
with our young
Prays with me when
our days begun

Listens to God
and reads his word
Follows the father,
and leads the herd

Walks right beside me
So I'm not behind
That type of man
is hard to find

So, if you find him,
Please send him my way
In Jesus name
I pray

Amen

Prayed For You

I knelt in quiet solitude
And whispered prayers into the night
For you, the one my heart adores
For someone who would treat me right

My Lord, a witness to my plea
Illuminated our destiny
I prayed for love to find its way
To weave our paths to meet one day

Like an answered prayer, you came to be
A miracle meant for only me
Your smile, like a melody divine
Your very being became a sign

In Lovers bliss, we reside
Two souls whose destinies collide
I prayed for you, and God replied
In lover's grace, forever mine

Fragrance of Your Favor

I have inhaled
The fragrance
Of your favor
In plain sight
And which you were
Likely saving for
One's true love;
Pardon me
It was destiny's making
So lovely
And so pure

Rainbow

After the rain, comes a rainbow
And there is nothing more beautiful
than that rainbow
All those bright, vibrant colors,
coming together to form
something so perfect
So promising
Those stratified hues
that lifts people's spirits
after the sky is done crying
Through all that darkness
comes such a marvelous light
And the young man that stands beneath it
he is just as lovely a creature
His deep brown eyes
hold the answers to every mystery
that our world has
He is breathtaking
How could you not help but to love him?
I stand there in astonishment,
pondering how two perfect things
could coexist in such a world
There is nothing more beautiful than that rainbow
Nothing more beautiful than you

MJ

In the moonlit jazz club, Michael played
His fingers danced across keys
Serenade
Notes flew like fireflies
In harmonious ties
As love's melody bloomed
My heart stayed

Into the Infinite

Together they dance, creations embrace
Jada's metaphors find refuge in his chords
Michael's notes find purpose, a tender grace
Their love, a canvas painted with vibrant words

Let them sing their words to the universe, these two
Falling in love was imminent
Their love a sonnet in twilight's hue
Forever echoing into the infinite

Captivating

He is so bold
It is scary; yet refreshing
I want to speak to him.
Be absorbed in his boldness
Be engulfed by his personality
I want to be tangled in his mind
Plucked by his vocal chords
I want to flow through his body
Like a symphony.
Be the brightness of his smile.
I just want to be a part of him…

Joyful

Your laughter
a symphony of notes
Each one distinct
harmonizing with hope

In the rhythm of your quirks
I find delight
A dance of contrasts
day into night

Star Crossed Lovers

Miles apart
Yet hearts combined
In lover's grace
Our souls aligned

Through texts and Facetime
We connect
A bond so strong
We both protect

The nights are lonely
The days are slow
But still our love
Does surely grow

I count down the days
Until we meet
Where distance fades
A love so sweet

Though far away
You're always near
In every chat
You reappear

I dream of days
When this is done
With distance gone
We become one

Hard to Love

I made it hard for you to love me
A maze of thorns and shadows
Yet you persisted, gentle and unwavering
Finding beauty in my broken pieces

Your love, a light illuminating my darkness
Guiding me through my own tangled maze
And in your eyes, I discovered grace
A redemption song for my wounded heart

Easy to Love

Falling in love with you was easy
Like leaves succumbing to the autumn breeze
Your laughter, a melody that danced in the air
Your eyes, a shining sun guiding me there

We wove our dreams with passion
In whispered wantings and sun-kissed trust
Each heartbeat echoed a promise unspoken
A love story sketched in the sky, unbroken

Your touch, a gentle rain on thirsty soil
Nourishing my roots, tender and loyal
As seasons change, our love remains
An eternal flame, no storm could wane

So here we stand, your hand in mine
Our souls dance together, forever aligned
Falling in love with you was easy, clear
For you are everything I have always held near

Air

You feel like air
Omnipresent
Refreshing
Always aware

You feel like air
Wrapped around me
In every direction
Proving that you care

You feel like air
Filling my lungs
With your love
and the kindness you share

I feel like air
Like I'd never truly lived
Until I breathed you in

I Waited for You

I waited for you
For my pink bonnet to be fitted
underneath your arm,
puzzle piece
Quickly turning into snores
that bounce off my freshly washed face
and lands on your chin

Cerulean

My Heart
Is Colored
In
Your
Hue

Equality

The sun
Comes out
To see
Your face

Nothing more
Lovely
Could replace

The Moon
The Stars
Stare
In disgrace

Longing for
Your sweet
Embrace

Intimacy

Skin against skin
We find our place
Souls collide
No empty Space

Your lips brush mine
Wild and free
Breaths collide
Like poetry

You caress my petals
Soft and warm
I rub your stem
Until you transform

I take a deep breath
As we combine
You inch in slowly
I arch my spine

As our eyes lock
A covenant is made
To let the fire
Consume us, unafraid

Our bodies entwine
And desire surges
Pleasing each other
Of our urges

As we reach our peak
Our hearts unite
Between the sheets
A love takes flight

You cover me with your body
Scantily clad
You're still the best
I've ever had

Love

Thou art
What stirs
Within Me

My Love

My love for you
is like a blast of emotion
From the very furnace
Of my heart

Your eyes
Are like coffee swirling
Into which I see infinity

Your lips
Are supple and sweet
Like the finest wine

Your skin
Is creamy smooth
Scented of shea butter
And coconut oil

To be with you
I would move
The Sun
The moon
And the stars

Please my love
Will you be with me
Tonight?

I Crave You

I can feel the tensions rising
It is getting hard to think
I really need to see you
You have me on the brink

I am loving all your features
I am feening on your style
You are all across my brain
I need to see your smile

Into the Depths of Your Ocean

Diving into the depths
  Of your ocean
      Felt safe
         Natural
            Acclimating myself
                To the increasing pressure
                    Of loving you so deeply
              Swimming through your mind
          As my soul intertwines with yours
    Forever to be tangled
In a mess of passion
 Trust and comfort
     Floating in the pools
        Of your coolness
           Surrounded in all degrees
              By your breezy
           Conversation
      Sinking slowly
    And surely
  Into purposeful
And everlasting
  Romance
     Never to view
        The surface again

Black Man

In between the heart and mind
You stand so grand and true
A beacon of sheer brilliance
In everything you do

Your strength, a steadfast anchor
In seas both old and new
A testament to the power
That's found in being you

With wisdom that outshines
The stars in the vast sky
Each thought you share, a spark
That lights the questions "how" and "why"

Ambition in your spirit
Like eagles, you soar high
Chasing dreams with fervor
That never shall run dry

Your presence is a symphony
Each moment, a sweet note
In life's grand composition
On waves of time, we float

Your laughter, a melody
That in my heart, I quote
A rhythm to the madness
A calming antidote

Amazing is too small a word
For all that you impart
For you are music in motion
A living work of art

In love with every facet
You've truly won my heart
Together, we're a masterpiece
A perfect counterpart

Younger Man

He is
Everything.
Checks off my list
Passionate
In every kiss
Sings to me
But something
Missed.

Rubik's Cube

I had a few
mixed-up colors
but I was OK

found cubes
colored closely to me.
Contorting myself
to try and help them turn around
and come closer to completion.
Getting myself
all mixed up
 in the process.

Fixing myself
was like getting all greens.
A win.
But still have a long way to go.
Yellow.
Closer but
not quite there.
Red.
OK, keep going.

Blue.
I was so close
to being done
And then I found you

and you
pointed out
that while I was almost done,
All sides nearly complete
There was a wrong color in every corner.

Perfection is Boring

I cannot say I have ever seen eyes
as captivating as yours
I get lost when I glimpse into the gift
That can only be described
as a prize from God himself

Every attempt to remove you
from my thoughts is a failure
As I scale your presence
throughout my cerebral cortex

And I lose my breath from trying to
Match my heartbeat to yours
And my pulse soars
because you remembered my name
And your frame, I am ashamed
for I am just a lame in comparison

You are perfection.
And I melt when you smile
In my direction.
May I bathe in the rays
Of your golden skin?

For your smile makes my days
Worthwhile
I would follow you into the Nile
For miles, I swear
As long as you are there

Nothing else can compare
To the joy and pain
That I gain when I see
Your name light up
On my screen

My thoughts become serene
As my pulse begins to slow
In the back of my head, I know
That I will never be more to you
Than some regular hoe

Performer

When he holds me
I feel
Compassion
And
Genuine
Interest
Radiating from his body
I like to think
That I know
Everything
About him
Except
For the secrets
Kept in the depths
Of his person
Behind the orchestra pit
And the drawn curtain that reads
"That is all"

Was Lost, but Now I am Found

I Felt Such a Terrible Longing for Him
I Imagined His Torment
It Stiffened My Knees
Cactuses And Crooked Trees
Wildflowers
His Peculiar Blood
I Felt Tortured
But He Won't Know the Difference
The Wounds Were Dark and Grim
But They Felt So Right
Hated...
Beautiful.
He Will Love Me
"You Have Faith?"
Yes.
"You Have Confidence?"
No.

You Taught Me

You taught me
How to live with
Purpose
Exposing the throws
Of my anxiety
And depression
And giving me a new
Direction
You taught me
How to pray
Without ceasing
Never decreasing
My faith
You taught me
How to chase my dreams
No matter how outlandish
They seem
You taught me
How to live with myself
How to master my health
How to succeed in stealth
You taught me
How to get what I need
And to do it without greed
Because I needed to feed
My desires
You took me higher
Than I'd ever flown
Into the unknown
And I'd never have grown
Without you

Melody of Love

In the quiet of the concert hall
Where pictures dance upon the walls
I found myself entranced by sound
A symphony of love unbound
His fingers brushed the ivory keys
A pianist lost in reverie
Each note a whisper, tender, true
And I, a captive in his tune
His eyes, like galaxies aglow
Held secrets only music knows
And when he sang, the stars aligned
His voice a balm for hearts maligned
He strummed his guitar with gentle grace
And time stood still in that sacred space
His lyrics wove a tapestry
Of longing, passion, harmony
I watched him sway, lost in the groove
His rhythm pulling me to move
For love, it seemed, had found its muse
In chords that echoed, souls transfuse
And as the final notes took flight
I knew this love was infinite
For in his music, I found my home
A melody that forever roams

I am Home

You made me feel at home
With the grips that your lips
Held on mine
Your hand on my back
Leaving chills on my spine

You made me feel at home
Letting my opinions speak up
Dominating
Expressive
Captivating

Escaping from the cage
That my teeth held tight
Not allowing a single release
But you

You made me feel at home
My tears
My joys
My fears
My toils

Wiped their feet
Welcomed by your warmth
And tight embrace
Because you made me feel at home

So, I stayed

As the lights dimmed
As the air went cool
As your tides shifted
Because I thought I was at home

But I quickly noticed
My lips tightening
My light dimming
My affections being handed their coat
And escorted to the door

I clutched what of myself I had left
And stepped over the threshold
A wave of sadness covered me
Like a strong winter breeze

Difficult.
Necessary.
I felt full.
Disappointed.
Whole.

I thought you were my home

I was wrong

I am my home.

Go Find Less

You told me that I was easy to love
And then you loved me less
And less
Each day

Fire

He regarded her with a strange feeling in his chest
And she viewed him with a yearning desire
The bed they shared felt lumpy
And they never got back their fire

Growing Apart

In the shadows, I stand alone
A heart once vibrant, turned to stone
Your eyes, unfocused, never meet mine
To you, it's just a passing sign

I speak but my words fall like rain
Unheard and unnoticed, a harsh refrain
I reach out but my touch is air
While you're still blissfully unaware

To you, I'm just a fleeting thought
A love once cherished, now forgot
Yet still I hope, with sweet despair
That one day, you will truly care

Iced Out

It Hit me
Like
A
Chilled Breeze
At first.
Attempting to
Find comfort
In your smile.
Realizing
I had not seen it
In a while.
Forcing steps
Forward.
Following the
Mapped out roads
That led to
Your embrace.
Replaced
With a
Detour sign
Urging me
To take
Another
Path.
Gusts of wind
Leaving frosted
Warnings
Across
my shoulders.
The pain
Felt so
Familiar.

I persist.
Your disdain
For me
Covering the way
Like a coating
of nightfall.
Darker
than I expected
And
Faster than
My feet
Could carry.

You are Mean

You promised
to love me
And lied

You called me
Ridiculous
When I cried

April Showers

Shelter felt as hopeless as expecting flowers
to have been left at my doorstep
As your perceived burden of loving me
felt as big as the pill last swallowed
knowing that you'd rather live without me
than love me correctly

Arizona Downpour

Inconsistencies drip into my hand
Like the first few drizzles before a storm
The coldness of your gaze
Sends a strong icy breeze across my shoulders
And travels down my back
As I try to unpack how we had even made it here
When the skies were just clear
I quickly found myself stuck in a downpour
Of your resentment
So heavy I might as well be blind.
Unprepared.
Next time, I will check your forecast
Before I dare
have the audacity
to Exist

Hurricane Season.

I am faltering
Quavering
Seizing under pressure
Dizziness
Forgetfulness
Praying to get better
I am stressing
Undressing
pressing forward as I can
I am trying to stay afloat
But the storm has high demands
I look to you in solace
Hoping that you calm the seas
It seems you are just an agent
For you bring a stronger breeze

Do You Even Like Me?

Shelter from
your discontent
Seems as hopeless
as expecting
You to feel
joy
from my smile
Or warmth
from my embrace
Your burden of loving me
Must have felt as large as
The pill I choked on
Accepting that you would
Rather live without me
Than love me like
I deserved.

Do You Even Like You?

You never quite told me
How you were feeling
But you were upset when
I felt unappealing

Liar

Is it fair to be aware
of the glare in your partner's eyes
and consider it a disguise?
Or is it only okay
When it is happening to me?

I want to be fair
Because I care about us
And I know that I fuss
sometimes even cuss
And I am trying to trust
But I cannot

Musicians

We could write such beautiful music together
If only he was not such a flirt
I am not even sure if he was really feeling me…
Maybe he is pretending, maybe he is just playing me

Discontent

You always found discomfort
In my nature.
Too Sweet.
In my kindness.
Too Meek.
In my beauty.
Unique.
I am not yours
To critique

Deception

Deceit behind your eyes
Intentions impure
Claiming forever
When you were not even sure

Who Sent You?

You do not
Delight
In My
Smile

Space

The distance is increasing
As I am sure you are aware
The facts remain the same
You fail to even care

I wanted to be loyal
Wanted to stay true
I wanted to deserve to be
The only girl for you

I knew you were a player
But never could imagine
I would be the only one
Engulfed in this attraction

My Heart's Sonnet

Before the fates spit out their wine
Let all who love be turned to swine
And find ourselves eternal fate
Neither king nor fool nor mate to date

Though time moves further from my youth
We hear the lies believed as truth
The moon rests silently above
My heart sings out to you, my love

For though our end may cease to be
I will never regret your company
With these arms, I reach out to you
The battle within me leads me through

Despite the risk
I journey on
Know death will come
We'll both be gone

Smooth Criminal

You were exactly what I prayed for
You were kind and patient
Passionate
Ambitious
Brave

You taught me how to be vulnerable
You gave me dreams I had never had
You showed me that my life is not over
Being a mom is not a setback

You made me feel like I could do anything
And that there was not an excuse not to try
You made me want to be better
You called me out when I was not actively pursuing my dreams

You showed me how unfulfilled I was with my life
You taught me how to let go
How to stop letting anxiety and fear control me

I was afraid of failing
I was afraid of not knowing
so, I would not even try
And you will not let me just tell you something
You made me prove it with my actions

You let me vent
You helped me sort out my traumas
You called me out on my bullshit

But you did not comfort me
You would not speak life into me
You were not open
You used sex as an apology
You wrote off my feelings

And when I was at my lowest,
with my hand extended up,
begging for help
You stood there and made me pull myself out

I wanted to keep you forever
I wanted you to be mine

But you showed me how to live without you

And then you made me feel
like I had no choice
but to do
 just
that

Cheers To the Love of My Life

Here is to,
Loving someone
with all your heart
Then, realizing that its
C r u m b l i n g apart
And there is
nothing
You can do
To stop it

Simpatico

As much as you may mean to me
The facts were proven true
That though you are the one, to me,
I am not the one for you.

I Let This Happen

Most of the time
I do not even know
What to say.

I used to be
So good with words
But you
Took that away.

Pretty little woman
Sit still.
Do not talk.
Obey.

Too loud.
Too confrontational.
And too stuck
In my way.

I made
Myself
Small
For you.

Foolish

I cannot be
Me
Around you.

Nope.

What are we doing?
Is this working?

Pringle

Maybe I should be single
I do not need a man
Emotions stacked then tumbled
Like the pringles from a can

Maybe

Maybe I need to be alone
Maybe it is time to learn
Stop pouring into everyone
And love myself in turn

February 12th

Candy hearts crushed
Against the concrete
Tease me
Like a soulmate lost
thanks to an unexpected breakup

I Know My Worth

In the rhythm of my love-struck heart
Where memories linger and lovers' part
I faced a choice, sad and tough
To love myself or my old love

Once, we danced in close embrace,
Two souls aligned, two hearts in grace
But seasons changed, and storms swept through,
Leaving doubts and questions new

I traced the lines upon my skin
Each mark, a battle fought within
The mirror reflected both joy and strife
A canvas where I painted my potential life

I weighed the cost of holding on tight
To memories that felt so right
Yet, self-love called out to me,
"Embrace your worth, set your spirit free."

So, I chose myself— courageous me
Unraveling dreams of what used to be
I stepped away from the bittersweet past
Into the unknown, where healing could last

No more chasing the sound of love's refrain
No more drowning in what might remain
I gathered courage like petals in bloom
And whispered goodbye so my life could resume

For sometimes love means letting go
Reclaiming the me that we used to know
In choosing myself, I found strength anew
A love deeper and truer—the kind that grew

So here I stand, single and free
A survivor of love lost - finally me
I chose the path where self-love resides
And in that choice, my wounded heart thrives

I Love Me

On the path to self, I gently tread,
With love as my guide, no fear, no dread
Each step, a dance, a chance to see
The strength and beauty within me

My inner light, a flame so bright
Guiding me through the darkest night
In its warmth, I find my way
Loving myself, day by day

It's been 6 months

And I
Still
Cry
When I think
About you

Love's End

I don't hate you, nor hold anger
For love's end is not a defeat
I reclaim the fragments of my heart
Stitching them together, bittersweet

I can't look at you without pain
Yet within that ache blooms strength
I learned to love the spaces you left
Embracing self, at any length

I Saved You

Growing into the woman I am now
Showed me that you weren't the only problem
I didn't give you the best version of me
I didn't know I had better to give
But following your example
And healing all my wounds
Shows me that maybe
I saved you
By letting you go

You Saved Me

Looking back at the me, I was,
When I had you
I would have been
Frustrated too

You gave me the keys
You left me clues
For me to be happy
Just like you.

I thought you were harsh
That you did not care
But you cared too much
Now I am aware

I am healed now
I found myself
And it was all
Because of your help

I listened to you
Finally
I took the notes
I used the key

The Jada I am now
So proud to be
Is only because
Of your love for me

Free

I had to set
Myself free
To truly become
A better me

Healing

I loved you once, with tender grace
Our hearts combined through time and space
But as seasons shift and wind patterns change
I chose to evolve, not to remain

I love you still, but hear this plea
I didn't change for you; I changed for me
The feeling of self I built with care
Became hopes of freedom in the air

I've grown, like tree roots seeking streams
No longer lost in one-sided dreams
The mirror reflects a stronger me
A love that's genuinely free

So here I stand, both scarred and whole
A symphony of growth through
heart and soul
I release you, not in bitterness or strife
But because I've learned to love my life

Self-Explore

I had to set myself free
Not from love, but from the illusion of we
For love isn't fancy dates or expensive cologne
It's the depth that's within our souls

I had no expectations, no threats of old
To find the love that's genuine, bold
No longer defined by another's gaze
I learned to love my mysterious ways

In the mirror's reflection, I saw it clear
Love is about releasing fear
It's about becoming, evolving, and growing
A dance where authenticity keeps flowing

And so, I loved you, but I loved me more
Not in selfishness, but in self-explore
I became a better version of my heart
A canvas where love and freedom start

Gone

I wanted to keep you
Wanted you to be mine
I had never experienced
A love so divine

I wish you never changed up
I wish our love stayed the same
It was so hard to leave you
But my heart still remains

I am glad to have met you
That you were part of my life
And now that you are gone
I do not live the same strife

You always pushed me
To follow my dreams
To not let life stop me
To grab life by the seams

Your voice still haunts me
It urges me on
I still cannot believe
That you are actually gone

Longing

What do I do with this longing?
My heart feels a sense of belonging
It urges you back, for a second chance
Yet still, my grief is prolonging

Too Little Too Late

I think about everything
that he does wrong
and it makes me think
about everything that you did right.

Cuffing Season

Fall leaves drift down
Resting quietly against the cobblestone
I sit alone in the stillness
as I Facebook stalk old lovers.
How did I get here?

Behind

You showed me love
In a way I had never
experienced before

You have in you
Traits that I have not found
In anyone else

You made me feel
Like I mattered
And I truly fell deeper
In love than I have ever felt

Nothing felt as good
As loving you
And while you
Showed me that a
Near perfect man
Does indeed exist

I have learned
From your absence
That I may never
Find that again

And if I had known
That you were
Actually
One of a kind

I would have
never
Left your love
Behind

Glass Half Empty

You tried to pour into me
Into a glass half empty
But there was a hole
In my cup

I Need a Chiropractor

My muscles
hold the memory
of your touch

Hollow

You used
To fill
My
Empty
Spaces

Deserve

You were my air
You were my home
You were my king
We shared a throne

Now that we're done
I'm lost without you
Why didn't I deserve
A love so true?

Phoenix, AZ

The road ripples in the heat
Like a rope of asphalt
While my tires howl
My coffee grows cold
And my eyes fight the passing of the sun
Ahead a stranger who looks like you
Pauses for the dusk's dark embrace
Only two hundred more miles to Phoenix
Where I lost the love of my life

Encore of Eternity

In dim-lit venues, where notes align
I found you – the composer of my heart's design
Piano keys caressed by your tender touch
A symphony woven in your clutch

Your nimble fingers, like crochet spun
Pluck melodies from chords, one by one
Each chord resonates within my core
Our secret language, forevermore

Our love danced to syncopated beats
Staccato kisses on music sheets
In spotlights glow, you boom, ignite
A whirlwind of desire, notes taking flight

Behind closed doors, we compose our fate
Our bodies harmonizing, love's final state
You whisper lyrics across my skin, so long
As I become your favorite song

Getting over you? It is simple, they say
But a love like ours will not fade away
I will write us an encore, a symphony divine
Where every note stretches across time

I Fear

You are hard to forget
Damn near close to perfect
Simply one-of-a-kind
The love of a lifetime

No matter what I do
My mind leads me to you
To the promises we made
To the love that will not fade

When I lay down in bed
You are the voice in my head
Telling me just to wait
That this still could be fate

But I know that is not true
Your affections withdrew
Yet my love remains still
I fear it always will

Whispers of Longing

On moonlit nights, I search the air
Tracing the memories of your lingering stare
God, once a witness, is silent above
As I yearn for your touch, lost and in love

The room echoes with your laughter's refrain
A haunting memory of what we could not sustain
Your footsteps whisper fading into blue
Will not lead me back yo you

I gather shards of our fractured past
Each piece a memory of love that did not last
The scent of your skin, the taste of your kiss
They cling to my soul, an ache I cannot dismiss

I pen poems as letters in the still of the night
Words that ache to fix our broken light
"Come back" they beg, ink bleeding my plea
But the paper remains blank, like a love lost at sea

Getting over you? I do not know if I can
It has been one year, and you are still in demand
Notes of longing crescendo, seeking resolution
As I yearn for your return, the only solution

Ode To Roses

Roses weep tonight
Forever ruined
This I know
For they mock my very existence
The stars above have been swallowed
By the dark of the night
My heart burns with a secret
It has but one question for you
Why did you leave?
For without you, my beloved
The earth will continue to spin
However, far less enjoyable

Taurus

Was having a boyfriend
That was emotionally unavailable
Really such a terrible thing?
I mean yes, he was nonchalant
And made me cry
A lot
But at least
My nails
Were done

Bare

Across the vast country
My cupboard is bare
Along the yellow brick road
The footsteps of despair
Lead me to you

Fade

I asked God why
As the years go by
My love for you just will not fade
Would it be better
To cry you a sweater
Than pretend our love
Could be swayed

Tales of Regret

And though time breeds silence
Tales of regret
Michael, my love
I will never forget

Unwritten

You asked me to write you a poem
So, I wrote you an entire book
Hoping that one day you will read it
And your heart will become overtook
I know that I was the one that left
But I regret that every day
I do not have the courage to tell you
But your love, I long for in every way

Break My Own Heart

Maybe God knew what he was doing
When he pulled us apart
Forcing me to
Break my own heart

Because if you were
The one who'd left
I think that I'd have
Run out of breath

Michael

Might as well come back to me
I hear my heart call to you earnestly
Can I see your face again?
Hearts that break can also mend
All I dream about is you
Ever so hoping you're in my view
Let me hear you miss me too

Familiar

Do I miss you because your pain was familiar?
Or do I miss you because your love was the best thing I have ever experienced in my life?

Loved You Better

I should have loved you better
In moments when time slipped through our fingers
When laughter danced on the edge of our lips
And your eyes held depths I failed to explore

I should have loved you better
When storms raged within your soul
And I stood on the shore, silent
Instead of diving into the tempest with you

I should have loved you better
When your heart whispered secrets
And I chose deafness over vulnerability
Missing the symphony of your unspoken dreams

But now, in the quiet echoes of regret
I reminisce on what could have been
A mosaic of missed chances and faded sunsets
As I ache for the love I should have given

Yet perhaps love, like light, bends time
And in some parallel universe, I hold you close
Whispering promises against the wind
Where "should have" transforms into "always did"

Closure

I reached out
A year too late
Hoping to rewind
To bring back fate

I could not forget you
You stayed on my mind
I wrote you this book
It transcends time

Every day when
I read this back
It reminds me of
the love I lack

I regret every argument
Moments when I was displeased
For more time with you
I would pray on my knees

These years without you
I have healed from my wounds
I just wish this improvement
Led me back to you

I was not the best girlfriend
I had been abused
You were always so patient
Never made me feel used

You took care of me
And you loved my son too
He mentions you sometimes
He must miss you too

It overjoyed my heart
To talk to you again
You may not love me anymore
But maybe we can be friends?

Forgotten Memories

I thought I had healed

I had forgotten how bright
the twinkle in your eye
when you heard an
interesting chord or
an impressive beat drop

I had forgotten how
you smelled once the
Shea butter and
coconut oil
had settled
on your skin

I had forgotten how
calming your
presence was
and how much I
bathed in the coolness
of your disposition

I had forgotten how
much my love for you
had soared-
higher than I could see
with bare eyes

I had forgotten…
Until I slipped
back into your embrace
like I had never left

Like a melody
Playing on repeat
that I cannot
get
out
of my head

Midnight Summer Air

Laying on the beach
In the midnight summer air
Feeling the water hit our feet
With your interested stare

Taking me in, up and down
From my locs down to my feet
Forgetting about the history
Like it's the first time that we'd meet

Gazing into your deep brown eyes
Then to your dazzling smile
As you tell me I'm beautiful
And that you plan to stay a while

Gently grabbing my hand
And lacing your fingers between mine
Slowly leaning into me
As I feel a stop in time

Wrapping your arms around my waist
And pulling me to your face
Holding me like you crave me
And rebuke the empty space

You give me a little grin
And place your hand upon my chin
Easing me closer to your lips
Embracing skin to skin

And just like that we're locked in love
Our lips caught in a dance
Your hands all over my body
While my heart is in a trance

Minutes pass, but we don't care
Not breaking even for breath
Consuming all of each other
Until there's nothing left

I can't believe we ended up here
With me back in your embrace
But there's nothing I've wanted more
Than to be back in this place

You Found Me

In kisses soft through the moonlit night
Through gentle touch and gaze so bright
Two hearts in passion beat as one
Their wordless bond, like the setting sun

In closeness, not just flesh, but soul
A dance of lust, where glances stroll
They find a rhythm, sweet and slow
And in that place, their feelings show

With every breath, a silent vow
In moments past, they find their now
To hold each other, come what may
Their intimacy sparks their fears away

For love is more than touch, it's trust
In every laugh, in feelings gushed
A sanctuary built for two
It's love's own language, pure and true

Blue

I thought falling back into your arms
Would be the best choice
But I'm finding that I still can't use my voice
I told you I loved you ever still
But you won't tell me how you feel
Rekindling was great, a fairytale
But now my hope is down a well
How will I know if this is true?
Your lack of action leaves me blue
When we first started dating,
You intensely pursued
But now it feels like you're subdued
I'm not the type of girl to chase
Could you help me find my place?

Opposites Attract

Opposites attract like dark and light
Vision fixed on you when you're within my sight
Loving you is a win, I could never lose
If I had a choice, it would still be you I'd choose

There is no confusion, neither up nor down
I cannot help but smile when it's you around
Tell me what you're feeling, are you out or in?
I'm ready to start, do you want it to end?

Tell me if I'm hot or cold, am I wrong or right?
There's no nuance here, it's either black or white
I could be the air that flies beneath your kite
We could go together like the day and night

If you do not want this, I won't be happy, sad
It would not be good, but it would not be bad
Polarity could change, and for that I can't be mad
I would just be grateful for the time we had

Love Still Remains

I do not want to be friends
for friendship is a lie
A veil that hides the fire within
the longing that will not die

Let us not linger in the shallows
where friendship masks our aches
Let's dive into the depths, my love
where passion's waves awake

Let's abandon platitudes
discard the friend zone's chains
and continue to write our fairytale
where our love still remains

Second Chances

I used to follow your every lead
Supported your every wish
But still, we would end up at odds
With something always amiss

I was actively in therapy
Dissecting my inner parts
Learning to take my shattered pieces
And turn them into art

The more I began to find myself
The more that we would fight
It's as if the more I tried to heal
The more it was not right

I loved you but I had to leave
To truly begin to grow
But through that journey, I longed for you
More than you will ever know

And when I realized that my love
For you was holding on
I knew I had to at least try
To find what once was gone

I did not expect for us to pick up
Right where we left off
But seeing you again was easy
It was like no time was lost

I loved the way you looked at me
That goofy love-struck face
It gave me hope that one day
I could take my rightful place

I lost you once, and I did not think
That I would lose you again
But it truly took me by surprise
When you wanted to be just friends

Because friends do not look at you like that
Friends do not kiss into the night
Friends do not hold each other close
Being friends does not feel right

How could you cradle me in your arms
After all this time
And not feel all the love I do?
Why can't we just rewind?

You told me I was beautiful
You said you had missed my voice
You gave me what I wanted most
Then you made the wrong choice

I'm truly disappointed
But I know my worth
You cannot be mine
And that really hurts

But now that I know
That you are really gone
My only choice now
Is   to   move   on

Lovers And Friends

I cannot be your friend
And I do not want this to end
But I cannot be in your life
If I cannot be your wife

This summer has been great
But it seems you still cannot see
Whether or not it's me
With whom you would like to be

If there's one thing I have learned
My affections should be earned
You have got to put in work
Or it is just going to hurt

And no matter how deeply
I love you with all of my heart
I deserve someone to
Love my every part

It feels like you do not know
Which way you want to go
So I've got to make that choice
I have to use my voice

It should not be a fight
So this just can't be right
I love you, that is true
But I cannot be with you

Imagination

I didn't make this up, I swear
He gave me hope, I saw him there
He asked me out, we went on dates
We laughed together and called it fate

He held my hand around the park
He came to see me after dark
We hung out all night; it was on-brand
He even shook my daddy's hand

He smiled at me and said he felt healed
He missed my mama's home-cooked meals
He ran his fingers through my hair
He kissed me like he'd missed it there

He called me every single night
I told him that "us" just felt right
We slept together, cuddled close
When I craved it, he gave me a dose

He picked me up, spun me around
He made me moan, the sweetest sound
He wrapped my legs around his waist
When he wanted a deeper taste

He sold me dreams of trips together
Said he'd relocate closer, from Arizona weather
He even asked me to visit him back home
Because after he left, we felt alone

Days turned into weeks, and he grew colder
Warm embraces turned to the cold shoulder
I tried to hold on with texts and calls
Until he finally stopped answering them all

Then suddenly, he wants to be just friends
But how could our romance end?
Was what we had a fabrication?
Was it just in my imagination?

Just A Fling

Why did you let it go this far?
Why did you make my heart sing?
Why did you treat me so lovingly,
If this was just a fling?

I Thought That I Could Do This

I thought that I could do this
I thought that I could be
The type of woman you wanted
The one I'd grown to be

I thought that since I'd had this year
To truly grow and change
I'd finally deserve your love
Because mine still remained

I've healed and now I'm ready
I'm beauty and I'm grace
But I didn't think I'd have a chance
Until I saw your face

The fact that you still liked me
The way your eyes met mine
The moment when you gripped my waist
Your smile so divine

The late night when you asked me out
To lay with you on the beach
Kissing as the Sun came up
A memory to keep

I told you I still loved you
You said my smile healed
But though you swept me off my feet
You won't share how you feel

You said you needed to work on you
And I truly understand
That's why we broke up in the first place
Because I needed to take a stand

But though I'm glad to see your name
Lighting up on my screen
It's reminding me of what I do not have
A love that's just unseen

You still won't tell me how you feel
And the distance is increasing
I'm trying my hardest to hold on
My love is never ceasing

If you didn't love me back
I don't know what I'd do
But since you haven't said it back
I can't believe you do

I'm stronger, and I'm wiser now
I'm bolder, and I'm brave
As much as I may want this
I can't wait for you to change

It's time for me to let this go
I'm happier when I'm alone
I'm sorry to have to leave you again
But I cannot just be your friend

Danny Phantom

I could feel your spirit fading away
When your phone calls ceased its ringing
When your texts slowed their dinging
And your voice stopped its singing
in my ear

I could feel you losing interest
When you stopped checking on me
And only reached out to vent
When our daily conversations turned into
Every other day good morning's and goodnight's

I've been hurt before
So I picked up on every small change
In your disposition
Every compliment unmade
Every promise ungave
Every story portrayed

When "I want to hear your voice" turned into
"I don't feel like talking"
When "I want to see you" turned into
"I don't like taking pictures"

I'm not stupid
But I'll be delusional for you
If it means I don't have to accept the fact
That you're clearly only keeping me around to
boost your ego
and cure your boredom

But I am surprised
Because what I did expect
Was for you to slowly slip away
What I did not expect
Was for you to show up in my city
Unexpectedly
And tell me that you need to see my face
Just to stand me up
And never reach back out again
I supposed you would want to be friends
At some point
Instead of lovers
I didn't expect you to want to be nothing
With no notice
What I expected was for you to be
At least a little bit considerate of my feelings
What I did not expect
Was for you to break my heart a second time

Because you proved what I felt the first time we were together
You proved that you never truly gave a shit about me
You showed me the type of man you truly are
And I will not fall for your tricks again

Resentment

I thought all of this growth I made
Would lead me back to you
It hurts more than you'll ever know
For that to not be true

It felt like fate that you came back
And held me close again
It broke my heart when after that
You just wanted to be friends

I'm letting go, I promise
But that's just so hard to do
Because what we had was recent
What we did was something new

I longed to hear your voice
And feel your hands across my skin
I yearned to press your lips to mine
And to taste your kiss again

You fell into me naturally
Our connection effortless
And after that, I'm wanting more
While you are wanting less

You went back to Arizona
And I'm still here soaking wet
In a downpour of inconsistencies
Under a cloud of resentment

Honesty

I'm not even that pissed that you ghosted me
I'm hurt that you couldn't just tell me how you felt
While I was willing to do anything for you
You wouldn't do something that simple for me

Served Your Purpose

And even though you broke my heart
I still note you for my growth
If you hadn't shown me how to thrive
I would have never gotten close

Watching you pursue your dreams
Made me want to chase mine
And now I have this book series
With my name on the dotted line

I didn't ask for inspiration
All I wanted was your love
But after all you put me through
I think that was enough

That year without you changed me
In more ways than I can express
In terms of exes and baggage
I will admit you were the best

Usually, in my relationships, they leave me worse for wear
But you left me intact, even if you didn't care
When I left you the first time, I was sad, but I was whole
I didn't plan to have to leave again; that wasn't my goal

But healing has a way of making your life work
I can't hold on to you anymore; I have to put me first
I walk away in confidence; I strut my stuff with joy
On to better things, to a life I can enjoy

Now I Know

I love me more than I love you
That's why I had to see this through
I knew I wouldn't let you go
As long as I didn't know

And even though this broke my heart
The knowing gave me a fresh start
I can move on, knowing that I tried
And leave behind the tears I cried

Power

The thing about you finding me healed
Is that I'm honest now about how I feel
And what I'm feeling is surprised
I never thought that you'd be my demise

But you can't break me; you don't have that power
I'll continue to bloom, just like a flower
I'll take this loss and carry on
Even if it hurts me that you're gone

Just A Boy

I don't know if I'll ever see
Why we weren't meant to be
This hit me like a moving truck
Why do I have such bad luck?

I will never understand
Why you don't want to be my man
But since you don't, I will be clear
If you change your mind, I won't be here

I love myself; I know my worth
And even though this truly hurts
I'll pick up all my broken parts
And turn them into a piece of art

I've healed enough to not linger on
You made your choice, and now I'm gone
You could never take my joy
After all, you're just a boy

Mystique

Was it the pain I loved, or was it you?
Because now that we are done
I think I finally understand
Why you were not the one

You never spoke life into me
You never apologized
You withheld affection
You got upset when I cried

You made decisions without consulting me
You didn't show me off
You wouldn't help me when I asked you to
You wouldn't bless me if I coughed

You weren't open about your feelings
And you always kept me guessing
Our relationship wasn't stable
And it always left me stressing

I thought I wasn't good enough
I felt like you deserved better
It made me extremely insecure
Aiming to try and fix your displeasure

No wonder I needed therapy
Of course, I had to heal
I got caught in a vortex
Of what I thought was real

And now that I have grown and changed
I'm no longer a chain on your link
And suddenly, you're disinterested
Because I can feel and think

You wanted me when I needed you
You loved me when I was weak
And now that I'm beautiful AND powerful
I won't fall for your mystique

You Didn't Change

The sad thing is that you didn't change
You came back, treating me the same
Like I was a thing and not your girl
A temporary fixture in your world

I get why you don't want me back
Because now I'm demanding what you lacked
A relationship that takes real work
Not a fragile girl that puts you first

I deserve a husband, a family
A man who gives consistency
Someone who loves me endlessly
A man who has a plan for me

To you, I was just something to acquire
A pretty toy that you desired
Something that gave you confidence
You thought that I lacked common sense

You loved me when you thought I was weak
A little plaything you could keep
You can't deny it; you know it's true
I'm so glad to be done with you

The Five Stages of Grief

In twilight's hush
Where memories reside
Our laughter once boomed
Now a fading tide

Sunsets we painted
Full of wonder and grace
Now lost in the ocean
Gone without a trace

    Denial
Denial dragged me into the water, drowned
I clung to pieces of our love, unbound
Whispers of forever flowed through my veins
Reality cut deep, leaving stains

    Bargaining
I pleaded with God, begged for a rewind
To mend the frayed threads of fate, unkind
Promises whispered to the moon, aglow
But the world remained silent, letting go

    Anger
Anger surged, a war in my chest
Storms of resentment, loves final test
Why did you leave? Why this cruel silence?
Unanswered questions, your final defiance

Depression

In nights loneliness, tears flowed like rain
A river of sorrow, carving paths of pain
I mourned not just you, but the me we both knew
Your love was my lifeline, it made my skies blue

Acceptance

Dawn broke through the storm clouds, a fragile light
Acceptance snuck in, banishing the night
I held my broken pieces, tender and true
Healing began with self-love, anew

Intention

I just
Need
A night
To write

My Mouth is an Escape Room

What do you write about
When you have nothing to say
When all the words that are jumbled up
Keep getting in the way

When life and expectations
Of what I can produce
Are plenty more ambitious
Than what I can reduce

Struggling to say my piece
And wrangle in the thoughts
Are hopeless as a rodeo
That I had already lost

Failure before you begin
Is a hard pill to choke
Almost as big as the word vomit
That is wedged within my throat

A quietness you cannot escape
Not sure how you got stuck
Locked in a room that is full of clues
But cannot muster up a fuck

Silence

I SHALL NOT BE...
(silenced)

Bind your mouth and open your ears to hear what I must say
It is your time to listen, I will speak my mind today

Take a seat and prop your feet, open up your mind
Today's my day to open up and leave those fears behind

You think your loudness assists me because you must know right
But you will see what I am thinking on this dreary night

No please, sir, do not shift nor try to run away
You must sit here and be patient, on this blessed day

Do you not like what I am saying? Do you wish to move?
Though it may not fit in your world, staying might behoove...

I see you are trying to fight out words, why can't you just stop?
If I do not untie you now it seems as if you will pop....

Sadly, it must come to this, for you to care about my words
Forcefulness is blissfulness for you but that is absurd....

I am not the one that is hushed today I can now see
I am not blinded by your hatred now it is only me...

I would help you up into my soul and let you look around
When you get over yourself, you will see I am quite profound...

I shall not be (silenced)
I have changed though not sure how
I hope you are ready to listen because you cannot stop me now

Fading Notes

In the dim-lit room, where melodies once bloomed
We stood at a crossroads; our love doomed
His guitar lay silent, strings frayed and worn
As if relaying the chords of our love, now torn

He sang of passion, of moonlight and stars
His voice a haunting echo from afar
But love, like a fragile tune, can unravel
And our symphony faded, notes lost in the gravel

I watched him strum, lost in the song
His fingers dance on frets where memories belong
Yet the rhythm changed, discordant and cold
As if fate had composed a bitter tale untold

He whispered lyrics that once stirred my soul
But now they cut deep, leaving wounds so cold
The stage was our refuge, our sanctuary of sound
Yet it became a witness to love unbound

The applause faded, the encore never came
And we stood there, two broken hearts aflame
He packed his dreams, his melodies, and strife
Leaving me with memories of a love once full of life

The piano keys wept, the violin strings sighed
As we parted ways, our hearts heavy-eyed
For a musician's love is like a fleeting refrain
Beautiful, yet transient, like a passing summer rain

And so, I slipped away, like a note in the wind
Leaving behind the chords we could no longer mend
In the silence that followed, I found my release
A solo melody, a bittersweet peace

I am Found

Finding myself lost
On the drawn-out roads
That led to your heart
Did I misread a sign?
Did I misplace a part?

My journey was long
As I stayed on track
I gave it my all
There was no turning back

I yearned for your love
Though, your heart I do not see
It led me to a mirror
I was searching for me

Growth

Somehow
This year without you
Has turned me
Into exactly the person
You had always wanted
Me to be
Shame
It had to be
Without
you.

My Own

Finding comfort in your presence
Is not nearly as fulfilling
As finding comfort
In my own

Mr. Judge

Thank you
For teaching me
How to live
Without
You

My Own Song

His melodies lingered
Haunting my dreams
A symphony woven
With love's fragile seams

But I will rewrite the score
Find new rhythms to explore
And sing my own song
Somewhere I belong

Contents

Dedication
Introduction

Jada's Prayer	2
Prayed For You	4
Fragrance Of Your Favor	5
Rainbow	6
MJ	7
Into the Infinite	7
Captivating	8
Joyful	8
Star-Crossed Lovers	9
Hard To Love	10
Easy To Love	10
Air	11
I Waited For You	11
Cerulean	12
Equality	12
Intimacy	13
Love	15
My Love	15
I Crave You	16
Into the Depths of Your Ocean	17
Black Man	18
Younger Man	19
Rubik's Cube	20
Perfection is boring	21
Performer	23
Was Lost, But Now I am Found	24
You Taught Me	25
Melody of Love	26
I Am Home	27
Go Find Less	29
Fire	29
Growing Apart	30
Iced Out	31
You are Mean	32
April Showers	33
Arizona Downpour	33
Hurricane Season	34
Do You Even Like Me?	35
Do You Even Like You?	35
Liar	36
Musicians	36
Discontent	37
Deception	37
Who Sent You?	38
Space	38
My Heart's Sonnet	39
Smooth Criminal	40
Cheers to the Love of My Life	42
Simpatico	42
I Let This Happen	43
Foolish	44
Nope.	44
Pringle	44
Maybe	45
February 12th	45
I Know My Worth	46

I Love Me	47
It's been 6 months	48
Love's End	48
I Saved You	49
You Saved Me	50
Free	51
Healing	51
Self-Explore	52
Gone	53
Longing	54
Too Little, Too Late	54
Cuffing Season	54
Behind	55
Glass Half Empty	57
I Need a Chiropractor	57
Hollow	57
Deserve	58
Phoenix, AZ	58
Encore of Eternity	59
I Fear	60
Whispers of Longing	61
Ode To Roses	62
Taurus	62
Bare	63
Fade	63
Tales of Regret	63
Unwritten	64
Break My Own Heart	64
Michael	65
Familiar	65
Loved You Better	66
Closure	67
Forgotten Memories	67
Midnight Summer Air	71
You Found Me	73
Blue	74
Opposites Attract	75
Love Still Remains	76
Second Chances	77
Lovers And Friends	79
Imagination	80
Just A Fling	81
I Thought That I Could Do This	82
Danny Phantom	84
Resentment	86
Honesty	87
Served Your Purpose	88
Now I Know	89
Power	89
Just A Boy	90
Mystique	91
You Didn't Change	93
The Five Stages of Grief	94
Intention	96
My Mouth Is an Escape Room	96
Silence	97
Fading Notes	98
I am Found	99
Growth	100
My Own	100
Mr. Judge	101
My Own Song	101

About the Author
About the Series

About the Author

Jada Lasha Hollingsworth is a hopeless romantic who has fallen head over heels more times than she can count. Writing has been a passion of hers since she was a child, and after a big push from her Lord and Savior, Jesus Christ, she decided to turn that passion into a career. Jada is a native of Portsmouth, VA where she lives with her son, Jaden, and her adopted mixed-breed dog, Sarah. She spends her days working for an Animal Rights Nonprofit Organization and spends her nights twirling tales of love and loss. She received a Bachelor of Science in Interdisciplinary Studies with concentrations in English and Biology from Norfolk State University, an HBCU that taught her to take pride in her blackness and helped her find her voice as a writer.

○ YouTube – Jada Hollingsworth
○ Facebook – Author Jada Hollingsworth
○ Instagram – @Aesthetically_pleasing27
○ TikTok - @JadaLasha27

Also by Jada L. Hollingsworth

Limerence:
Confessions of a
Lovesick Middle Schooler

Infatuation:
Confessions of a
Lovesick High Schooler

Monophobia:
Confessions of A
Lovesick College Girl

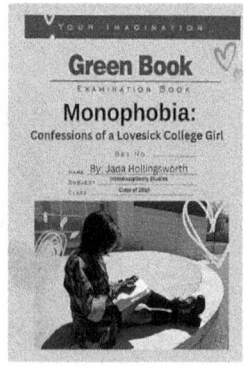

About the Lovesick Series

The Lovesick Series follows Jada Hollingsworth, the Lovesick Liaison, as she navigates the different stages of love throughout her life. The series begins with Limerence and continues through Infatuation, Monophobia, Cherophobia, and Emophila. Throughout the series, the author explores how various experiences shape our growth, transformation, and understanding of life and love.

What makes the Lovesick Series unique is that each book was written during the corresponding time period in the author's life, starting from middle school and progressing through high school, college, young adulthood, and parenthood. This approach makes each book a time capsule, providing an authentic glimpse into the emotions, experiences, and relatability of love at each stage. Each book covers a significant phase of existence and self-discovery, from crushes and relationships to trauma, heartbreak, loneliness, true love, and self-love.

The Lovesick Series invites readers to revisit and unpack their own life experiences by exploring the relatable and diverse ways in which they, too, have experienced love and loss. Through beautifully crafted poems, the series offers true transparency and vulnerability, providing chronological storytelling that resonates with readers.

Colophon

The Wider Perspectives Colophon page has been reworked and reworked to try to accommodate the ever growing list of authors represented. It is a reflection of the pen-to-paper and often aloud-presented talent in the Hampton Roads area of Southeast Virginia. This page used to have many cute and poetic expressions, but the sheer number of quality artists deserving mention has become some serious business. Voices shouldn't be silenced any more than experiences should be discounted. The book that will save your life is waiting for you from one of these authors!!

Luana LU Portales
Ken Sutton
Samantha Casey
Sonya Fitch
Chris (thePoeticGenius) Green
Donna Burnett-Robinson
Faith May Griffin
Se'Mon-Michelle Rosser
Lisa M. Kendrick
Brittiny Gardner
Charles Wilson
Cassandra IsFree
Nich (Nicholis Williams)
Samantha Geovjian Clarke
Natalie Morison-Uzzle
Gus Woodward II
Brandi Dise
Jack Cassada
Patsy Bickerstaff
Dezz
Grey Hues
(Doowrag) Daniel Garwood
Tabetha Moon House
Nick Marickovich
Madeline Garcia (Maddie G.)
Chichi Iwuorie
Rivers Raye
Symay Rhodes
Terra Leigh
Tanya Cunningham (Scientific Eve)
Raymond M. Simmons
S.A. Borders-Shoemaker
Taz Weysweete'
Ann Shalaski
Serena Fusek
Jade Leonard
Darean Polk
Bobby K. (The Poor Man's Poet)
J. Scott Wilson (Teech!)
Gloria Darlene Mann
Neil Spirtas
Edith Blake
Don (Bent Spoke) MacKellar
Jorge Mendez & JT Williams

Sarah Eileen Mendez (Williams)
Stephanie Diana (Noftz)
Shanya – Lady S.
Jason Brown (Drk Mtr)
Kailyn Rae Sasso
Crickyt J. Expression
Toni Lynn Britton
Morgan Guyton (Starchild)
Faith Clay (Arlandria Speaks)
Talis Matreshka
Luna Monet Sierra
Chris Will Hardy
Erato -the Muse (Oliver Chauncey-Heine)
Jason Williams Willy-Jay
Easter PoetikDesire Dodds

Crystal Nolen
Zach Crowe
James Harry Wilson
Catherine TL Hodges
Martina Champion
Kent Knowlton
Vanessa Jones
Tony Broadway
Maria April C.
Mark Willoughby
Linda Spence-Howard

the Hampton Roads Artistic Collective (757 Perspectives) & The Poet's Domain are all WPP literary journals in cooperation with Scientific Eve or Live Wire Press

Check for those artists on FaceBook, Instagram, the Virginia Poetry Online channel on YouTube, and other social media. Please check out how *They art*

www.ingramcontent.com/pod-product-compliance
Lightning Source LLC
Chambersburg PA
CBHW071955100426
42738CB00044B/3103